Pleasures of Summer

A Starbucks Coffee Cookbook

Foreword by
DAVE OLSEN

Text by
MARY TOWNSEND

Original Recipes by
JOHN PHILLIP CARROLL

Food Photography by
PHILIP SALAVERRY

Sunset
BOOKS

Sunset Books
President and Publisher: Susan J. Maruyama
Director, Finance & Business Affairs:
   Gary Loebner
Director, Manufacturing & Sales Service:
   Lorinda Reichert
Director, Sales and Marketing:
   Richard A. Smeby
Editorial Director: Kenneth Winchester
Executive Editor: Robert A. Doyle

Sunset Publishing Corporation
Chairman: Jim Nelson
President/CEO: Robin Wolaner
Chief Financial Officer: James E. Mitchell
Publisher: Stephen J. Seabolt
Circulation Director: Robert I. Gursha
Editor, *Sunset Magazine:* William R. Marken

Starbucks Pleasures of Summer
was produced by
Weldon Owen, Inc.
President: John Owen
Associate Publisher: Anne Dickerson
Project Coordinator: Genevieve Morgan
Assistant Editor: Jan Hughes
Art Direction and Design: John Bull
Designer: Tom Morgan
Assistant Designer: Larry Azerrad
Production: Stephanie Sherman
Map: Kenn Backhaus
Illustrators: Martha Anne Booth,
   Diana Reiss-Koncar
Copy Editor: Sharon Silva
Proofreader: Desne Border
Index: Ken Dellapenta
Writer: Norman Kolpas
Food Stylist: Sue White
Assistant Food Stylists: Tony Lamberto, Dan
   Becker, Sara Deseran, Bruce Yim
Prop Stylist: Amy Glenn
Photography Assistant: Beth Schneidler

First printing August 1995

ISBN 0-376-02614-6
Library of Congress Catalog Card
Number: 94-69948
Printed in the United States

For more information on *Starbucks
Pleasures of Summer* or any other Sunset
Book, call 1-800-634-3095. For special
sales, bulk orders, and premium sales
information, call Sunset Custom Publishing
Services at (415) 324-5577.

Starbucks by mail. Call 1-800-782-7282 for
a free catalog subscription and information
on how to acquire Starbucks coffee.

Foreword

*M*ary and Dave inspecting coffee beans in Guatamala.

One of the most marvelous things about coffee is that it affords us so many different kinds of pleasure. Personal indulgence. Everyday staple. Affordable luxury. Social lubricant. Quiet contemplation. Indeed, great, sometimes surprising things can happen when this age-old liquid passes the lips. As you make great coffee a part of your life, a new level of enjoyment becomes possible. No longer is it a mere generic drink. Each cup holds the possibility of yielding fresh discoveries—whether a new varietal coffee or blend or a new way or occasion to enjoy the beverage.

That spirit of discovery is the driving force behind this book, which deals specifically with coffee drinking during what is many people's most pleasurable time of the year, summer. And I can think of no better person to explore that topic than my colleague at Starbucks, Mary Townsend. Mary's job description actually states that she must travel the world in search of only the finest coffees. Her work brings her to the slopes of Mount Kenya; to small cooperatives on the mountainsides surrounding Lake Toba in northern Sumatra; to Kona on the big island of Hawaii; to anyplace where superior coffee can be found. In a career dominated by men, she has persevered through two and a half decades to become one of the best-known and most highly respected people in the coffee business.

A wonderful judge of coffee and a courageous traveler, Mary Townsend brings her warmth and exuberance to each new experience, sharing with anyone she meets the pleasures she finds in a cup of coffee. Please join her now in tasting summertime coffee at its best.

DAVE OLSEN

Contents

Summertime Coffee

Just as no two summer days will ever be exactly the same, the ideal cup of summer coffee will vary with your mood, with the occasion and with the weather. Some, like Costa Rica, are bright and lively—the perfect cup with which to greet the morning. Kona evokes tropical breezes and soft balmy nights. Mexico Altura is full of vibrant color, energy and fun, like a fiesta in July.

Other more exotic coffees, such as Kenya, Ethiopia and Arabian Mocha Sanani, offer tantalizing glimpses of the world's endless and remarkable variety. Blends, too, can be tailored to the specific needs of the season, such as Starbucks Gazebo Blend®, a good candidate for icing. Put simply, the world offers a grand tasting tour of coffee varieties ideal for summertime enjoyment. The following pages provide you with a detailed itinerary for that voyage of discovery, introducing you to the history, geography and culture of each nation that produces coffee suited to warm-weather pleasure.

The serial murals adorning the walls of a sixteenth-century church in Zege, Ethiopia, combine religious art and tribal lore, which often explores the symbiotic relationship between man and nature.

Ethiopia Sidamo & Yergacheffe

THE COFFEE:

Imagine breathing in the complex aromas of a huge bouquet of summer flowers and you'll begin to understand the pleasures of drinking these two varietal coffees from Ethiopia. Coffee beans from the Sidamo growing region in the south-central plateau have, when brewed, a penetrating floral fragrance with hints of spice and citrus zest. Partisans of coffee from Yergacheffe, a high-mountain town within Sidamo, find its perfumes more intense still. Pleasing body and acidity round out both coffees. Whether sipped hot or iced, Ethiopia Sidamo and Yergacheffe offer coffee experiences at once intoxicating and refreshing.

THE PLACE:

It seems only fitting that *Coffea arabica*—the coffee species that gives us the finest beans—should have originated in the same landscape where the earliest remains of mankind have been found, and where the Ark of the Covenant is reputedly hidden in a centuries-old Orthodox Christian church. Coffee trees still grow wild in Ethiopia. But the estimated 125,000 acres occupied by wild trees amount to only about one-eighth the amount of land under cultivation on coffee plantations, making Ethiopia the largest grower of arabica coffee in Africa. Coffee is so much a part of daily life here that its brewing and drinking have become ritual. In grand house and humble shelter alike, charcoal is first heated in a brazier. A single glowing coal

The Ark of the Covenant reputedly rests in an Ethiopian church such as this.

is plucked from the fire and a piece of incense placed atop it, filling the humid air with heavy smoke reminiscent of frankincense. In a symbolic act of purification, green coffee beans are rinsed with cold water poured from a jug. Then the beans are spread on a metal pan over the hot coals. The beans are stirred with a stick while they roast until they turn dark brown and their oils rise to the surface. As they roast, their aroma mingles with that of the incense.

With a wooden mortar and pestle, the roasted beans are pounded to a powder and poured into an earthen coffee pot half-filled with boiling water. As with the better known Turkish coffee, the mixture is brought back to a boil and removed from the fire three or four more times, then set aside for a few minutes to let the grounds settle.

Handleless cups barely bigger than a large thimble await on a low wooden table. The coffee is poured. Solemnly, guests sip and savor it, their cups refilled until no more remains.

THE LEGEND OF KALDI

According to Ethiopian legend, an old goatherd named Kaldi was tending his flock one day when he noticed his animals grew friskier after nibbling on the red berries of a wild shrub. Kaldi tried the berries himself, and felt invigorated and youthful. He brought them to a holy man, who suspected devilry at work and cast them into the fire. The resulting aroma made him change his mind, and the roasted beans were scooped from the embers, ground and infused in water to brew the first cup of coffee.

Above: A priest in the Ethiopian Christian order.
Below: Christmas Devices Dancers, Lalibela, Ethiopia

Gusala's Coffee Shop

*Here, the undefined boundary was at its clearest—the change from the
highlands of Ethiopia proper to the barren desert of the Somali tribes. And as
you left the green grass and the rocks, unexpectedly, you found a coffee shop.*

*It was a far cry from the coffee shops of the western world. It was merely a
small enclosure of thorn branches pulled into a careless circle, a defensive
perimeter called a zeriba, in which was a wood fire, a single chair carved out
of a solid trunk of thorn tree, and a piece of matting thrown over some rickety
sticks to provide a piece of shade. A little to one side stood the one-room mud
house of the owner, whose name was Gusala.*

❦

*In this coffee shop you were expected to bring your own drinking vessel,
and Gusala would make a thick black brew from wild coffee beans, standing discreetly in the background while you waited, and his wife, a cheerful,
buxom woman of thirty or so whose name was Shwaya, would stand at the
door of the house with her innumerable children gathered round her, all
silently watching, while the water boiled over the twig fire and the scent of
wood smoke hung in the hot air.*

ALAN CAILLOU, *SHEBA SLEPT HERE*, 1971

**Much of Ethiopia's Christian
culture is carefully preserved
in its open-air churches.**

Arabian Mocha Sanani

THE COFFEE:

If summer is your best season for contemplation, Arabian Mocha Sanani—hot or iced—may well become your coffee of choice. One of the world's most complex coffees, it combines lofty hints of flowers and winy, berrylike fruits with down-to-earth flavors that suggest rich-tasting nuts or the dark cocoa that has made the name *mocha* synonymous with the marriage of chocolate and coffee. Add its heavy, syrupy body and you have a coffee ideal both for drinking while you mull over other matters and for sipping and appreciating in its own right.

THE PLACE:

The name Arabian Mocha Sanani offers a capsule lesson in the history and geography of the coffee itself. *Arabian* refers to the Arabian peninsula, and more specifically to the mountainous southwestern portion facing Ethiopia across the mouth of the Red Sea, an area known in ancient times as Arabia Felix and today as North Yemen or the Yemen Arab Republic. Mocha comes from the coastal city of Al Mukha, the main coffee-shipping port until its harbor filled with silt about a century ago. Although most Arabian coffee is now shipped out of Hodeidah, some one hundred miles to the north, mocha still designates fine Arabian coffee. The best of these come from the high-altitude growing areas around the Yemeni capital of San'a, hence, the term *Sanani*.

At day's end in an Arab encampment, young and old alike gather to hear tales of the past,
to be followed by the ritual brewing of coffee.

In the Suq al-Milh in Yemen's capital city, San'a, a vendor (above) presents steaming hot flat breads for sale. Throughout the country, cities such as Shibam (opposite), some three hundred miles east of San'a, seem time capsules of the distant past.

Harvested today as they were more than fourteen centuries ago, the coffee cherries are allowed to dry on the tree, then a tarpaulin is spread below and the tree is shaken to dislodge the cherries. Crushing between two grindstones removes the dried hulls from the coffee beans.

For their own enjoyment, Yemenis grind their coffee to a powder and boil it with a little crushed cardamom. If they want it sweetened, they'll also add some sugar and powdered ginger. The spices are thought especially refreshing in the desert heat. Dried coffee hulls, separated from the beans, are infused along with cinnamon or ginger to make a tealike beverage called *kishr,* whose popularity in the harems of old Constantinople earned it the nickname "sultan-style coffee."

The Art of Coffee-Drinking

As with art 'tis prepared, one should drink it with art.
The mere commonplace drinks one absorbs with free heart;
But this—once with care from the bright flame removed,
And the leme set aside that its value has proved—
Take it first in deep draughts, meditative and slow,
Quit it now, now resume, thus imbibe with gusto;
While charming the palate it burns yet enchants,
In the hour of its triumph the virtue it grants
Penetrates every tissue; its powers condense,
Circulate cheering warmths, bring new life to each sense.
From the cauldron profound spiced aromas unseen
Mount to tease and delight your olfactories keen,
The while you inhale with felicity fraught,
The enchanting perfume that a zephyr has brought.

TADJ-EDDIN-AID-ALMAKNAB-BEN-YACOUB-MEKKI MOLKI,
QUOTED IN *CHRESTO MATHIE ARABE,* 1806,
BY BARON ANTOINE ISAAC SILVESTRE DE SACY

Breakfast in San'a

Light filtered into the city. The upper stories of a thousand-year-old stone building were touched by the predawn glow. A lead-colored light spread through the chilly depths of darkened passageways paved with blue-gray stone. The twisting laneways were nearly deserted, but as I moved through the shadows I could smell the smoke from household breakfast fires. . . . I moved further into the city, where rows of veiled women were selling loaves of steamy bread from cloth-lined tea chests. The wooden chests were covered with blankets to retain the heat. The freshly baked bread gave off a delicious aroma of barley and sorghum flour. I bought one of the five-inch-wide loaves and sat down in a streetside teashop to sip a thick foamy drink made from ground coffee husks and sweetened condensed milk. A crushed green cardamom pod floated on the surface. The sun was rising.

ERIC HANSEN, *MOTORING WITH MOHAMMED:*
JOURNEYS TO YEMEN AND
THE RED SEA, 1991

Kenya

The intricate beadwork of hand-made Kenyan jewelry reflects the rich colors of the country itself, including that of the vivid red volcanic soil in which the nation's coffee trees thrive.

THE COFFEE:

You're standing in a tropical garden, and every breath fills your head with the aroma of fruit-tree blossoms, overpowering yet fresh and bright. That's how I imagine the first experience of drinking a great Kenya coffee. Every sip that follows brings good medium body, concentrated fruit flavors recalling blackberries or black currants, and crisp, clear acidity reminiscent of good red wine—big, bold and dramatic. The bright acidity makes Kenya both a great coffee for serving over ice and a surprisingly refreshing hot brew. At its best, it's a truly regal coffee, standing above the other East Africans in flavor, consistency and intrigue.

THE PLACE:

Kenya coffee comes from a country filled with nature's treasures: the rarefied air; the red volcanic soil; the elephants, rhinos and giraffes; the lush highlands and dry, harsh bushlands; and the varied population of native peoples, among them the Kikuyu, Masai, Samburu and Luo tribes who are regal, proud and independent. My favorite country, it's a powerful, free land filled with colors and contrasts, where every day is an adventure. Missionaries first brought coffee cultivation here in 1901. Today, the Kenyans produce a world-class coffee that ranks alongside tourism—fourteen national parks attract hundreds of thousands of visitors each year—as the nation's chief sources of foreign exchange. Some 70 percent of total coffee production takes place on small, privately

A girl proudly wears traditional tribal attire at Kenya's Samburu Game Reserve.

WHY THE SUN SHINES SO BRIGHTLY

We have been told that the sun once married the moon. One day they fought, and the moon struck the sun on the head; the sun, too, damaged the moon. When they had done fighting, the sun was ashamed that human beings should see that his face had been battered, so he became dazzlingly bright, and people are unable to regard him without first half closing their eyes.

from *The Masai: Their Language and Folklore,* by A. C. Hollis, 1905

held farms, their terraced plantings following the contours of the steeply sloped landscape.

Kenya's coffee-growers are "a people, who are constantly thinking and talking of planting, pruning or picking coffee, and who lie at night and meditate upon improvements to their coffee-factories," in the words of Isak Dinesen, who vividly described her own plantation near Nairobi in *Out of Africa*. Indeed, a reading of the book provides a faithful and evocative account of the dedication with which Kenyan coffee was grown, harvested and processed between 1914 and 1931, and still is today. Yet, the Kenyans' unquestioned dedication is marked with irony. They themselves seldom drink their coffee, preferring tea—a legacy of British colonial times—made from locally grown black tea leaves, simmered for four to five minutes to produce a very strong brew and then lightened with just a little milk.

African Air

The chief feature of the landscape, and of your life in it, was the air. Looking back on a sojourn in the African highlands, you are struck by your feeling of having lived for a time up in the air. The sky was rarely more than pale blue or violet, with a profusion of mighty, weightless, ever-changing clouds towering up and sailing on it, but it has a blue vigour in it, and at a short distance it painted the ranges of hills and the woods a fresh deep blue. In the middle of the day the air was alive over the land, like a flame burning; it scintillated, waved and shone like running water, mirrored and doubled all objects, and created great Fata Morgana. Up in this high air you breathed easily, drawing in a vital assurance and lightness of heart. In the highlands you woke up in the morning and thought: Here I am, where I ought to be.

ISAK DINESEN, *OUT OF AFRICA*, 1937

Marabou storks gather atop a lone acacia tree in the Masai Mara Game Reserve.

Costa Rica Tres Rios

Decorating an ox-drawn wooden cart traditionally used in Costa Rica to carry coffee from the fields to the mill, a profusion of bright colors in an intricate design seems to symbolize the bright, lively flavors of the coffee itself.

THE COFFEE:

The best coffee from Costa Rica is typified by that of the Tres Rios—three rivers—region on the Pacific slopes of the high volcano-rimmed central plateau. It has big, bold beans, is always beautifully prepared and is one of Central America's most consistent and reliable coffees. I find it easy to enjoy, an underappreciated jewel with straightforward flavors and great, mouth-watering acidity. Such characteristics make a cup of Costa Rica Tres Rios an experience as bright, clear and uncomplicated as a summer morning. The early hours are, in fact, the ideal time to indulge in it, although you're likely never to tire of Costa Rica Tres Rios as the day goes on.

THE PLACE:

View the Tres Rios region when the coffee trees are in bloom, from late spring to late summer, and you'll understand why the locals describe the phenomenon as "Costa Rican snow." Small white blossoms smelling like jasmine blanket the dense groves of lustrous green leaves. And just as quickly as snowflakes vanish beneath the sun, so do the blossoms disappear within a few days of flowering, giving way some six months later to fully ripened red coffee cherries. My favorite coffee farm is in Tres Rios. When I am traveling in Costa Rica, I always stop to spend an afternoon there with the plantation owners, to look out across the farm's lush, green valley and down at the red-roofed mill and to talk of coffee and the world.

A painting by Otoniel Mejia records traditional ways of harvesting coffee.

WHEN SUMMER STAYED TOO LONG

Strange things began to happen in the town. The potatoes tasted like yams, the yams like papaya, the papaya like turnips, the turnips like tomatoes, the coffee bean while it was still green smelled like orange blossoms, daisies bloomed from rose bushes, gladiolus from tulips, and bougainvillea from lilies. Everyone realized that summer was staying around too long and it wasn't raining; there wasn't even a hint of rain in the sky, only chalky white clouds. But they didn't worry, because the river brought more water than ever and it was as soothing as the sea; it caressed them to sleep with caresses that were more creative, more imaginative by the day, as the river slowly carried out its journey.

from "When New Flowers Bloomed" by Carmen Naranjo, translated by Linda Britt, in *Costa Rica: A Traveler's Literary Companion*, 1994, edited by Barbara Ras

The profusion of plantations in Costa Rica today was actually built on a decidedly modest notion. The coffee tree's earliest introduction to the nation from Cuba in 1779 was as an ornamental shrub for patios and courtyards. The government, however, soon recognized coffee's commercial potential. In the early nineteenth century, every family was required by law to plant a minimum of two coffee trees in its garden. The government even provided the trees free to those who couldn't afford them, and land was also granted to anyone willing to raise coffee as a crop. Until fairly recently, most owners of small coffee farms transported their harvest to market in ox-drawn wooden carts painted in vivid patterns.

In 1843, William Le Lacheur, the captain of an English merchant vessel, docked at the port city of Puntarenas, Costa Rica. Needing ballast for his return voyage, he filled his hold with bags of coffee beans. Thus began a European fondness for Costa Rican coffee that continues to this day.

Tres Ríos ✩

There is no mountain more lovely than La Carpintera; there is no water more pure than the water of your springs; no air more clear than yours; no coffee richer than that of your hills and your slopes; no pathways fresher or prettier than yours. Nowhere in Costa Rica is there a place that surpasses you in natural riches; in jungles more filled with birds than yours; and, above all, no place more sacred, to me, than this land in which I took my first steps. . . . Now you have heard me: you have seen yourself, my own town, in my eyes, in my soul: you have understood that there is within my soul something of your countryside, of your waters, of your beauty. . . . For the love of my sweetest wife, for the love of my children; for that of my parents and brothers, do not doubt that I have never forgotten the light that my eyes took in during the first years of my childhood, the shelter of your mountains, the song of your rivers and the warbling of your birds.

MOISÉS VINCENZI, EXCERPTED IN *ESCRITORES DE COSTA RICA*, 1942, EDITED BY ROGELIO SOTELA, EXCERPT TRANSLATED BY NORMAN KOLPAS

Coffee trees blanket a high-mountain slope in the Tres Rios region.

Mexico Altura

THE COFFEE:

Grown on the verdant slopes of the high sierras in the southern state of Oaxaca, Mexico, Altura (literally, high-grown) beans yield a fragrant cup of coffee with occasional hints of earthy, nutlike flavor and a light, tart acidity. They make a bright, mild, satisfying brew that can be enjoyed hot all day long. I find Mexico Altura a delightfully uncomplicated summertime drink.

THE PLACE:

Coffee has been grown in the mountains and coastal hills of southern Mexico since the end of the eighteenth century, and while it remains today the nation's leading export crop—ranking Mexico third among the world's producers of arabica beans—the quality can vary widely. Some of the best comes from small farms high in the Sierra Madre del Sur of Oaxaca, a state now widely renowned for the flowering of its native crafts, especially fantastical, hand-carved wooden animals, angels and devils, all painted in a profusion of bright, swirling colors.

Most restaurants in Mexico today serve a fairly familiar cup of coffee brewed by drip filter or espresso machine. Any hint of bittersweet flavor is likely due to the sugar sometimes added during roasting to give the beans a shiny, caramel finish that many people south of the border prefer. For a more authentic Mexican coffee experience, visit a private home or a country inn for *café de olla*.

A detail from a mural entitled "Women with Flowers and Vegetables," by Diego Rivera.

The tile work of painter Ramos Martinez captures the tropical ambience of Mexico's coffee-growing areas.

In a large earthenware jug *(olla),* coarsely ground dark-roasted Mexican coffee is simmered in hot water with raw sugar, cinnamon sticks, whole cloves and orange peel. The result: a lively drink as warming and pleasing as Mexican sunshine.

In the Country

Let us laugh and sing beneath the green foliage
Where the sun drizzles down his light in trickles of gold;
Let us happily contemplate the pageantry of the countryside,
The babble of the river, the vastness of blue.

United is our song with the trilling of the birds,
The rustle of the leaves as they move in the wind.
Come, dear companions, and cut with our own gentle hands
The loveliest flowers that grace the garden.

Let us pour out our souls to the entire universe,
Which pulses in the bird, in the water, in the flower,
And with these splendors, we will create a poem
Most simple and beautiful in praise of God.

EARLY-TWENTIETH-CENTURY OAXACAN POET ELSA RODRIGUEZ, IN
FLORILEGIO DE POETAS Y ESCRITORES DE OAXACA, 1927, EDITED BY ALFONSO
FRANCISCO RAMIREZ, TRANSLATED BY NORMAN KOLPAS

A yarn-and-beeswax artwork by the Huichol tribe pays tribute to nature's bounty.

Located near Oaxaca, the ruins at Monte Albán suggest the intricate layout of an
ancient Mayan settlement.

Kona

THE COFFEE:

Close your eyes, take a sip of Kona coffee and you're instantly transported to the Big Island of Hawaii. Kona coffee is known for its aroma—delicate, yet interestingly complex, with fresh, citrusy tropical fruit and hints of caramel. The taste is gentle, smooth, even and mellow, with a light but lively acidity. The pleasures of Kona coffee are subtle and best appreciated hot in the cup; icing can make them seem to vanish in the air. But a cup of steaming Kona nonetheless evokes the radiating sun and a soft tropical breeze. You're enjoying a taste of paradise, as soothing as the islands themselves.

THE PLACE:

Coffee plants first came to Hawaii in 1825, when Chief Boki, the governor of Oahu, collected some in Rio de Janeiro and planted them on his land in the Manoa Valley. Two years later, the Reverend Samuel Ruggles planted cuttings from those trees as garden ornamentals on Kona. The cuttings thrived, and locals soon discovered that a twenty-mile stretch of rich land at an elevation of seven hundred to twenty-five hundred feet along the breeze-cooled slopes of the world's largest volcano, Mauna Loa, provided an ideal spot for growing coffee. Britons and Americans ran the first plantations, and they were followed by waves of Japanese, Filipino, Portuguese, Chinese and Micronesian immigrants, who have bestowed their diverse cultural traditions upon Kona coffee.

Coffee trees share the lush landscape with all kinds of tropical vegetation and other plants and flowers grown so dense they virtually hide them. Almost every day, gentle tropical rains fall; when I think of Kona's coffee fields, I can almost smell the rain

A Kona native displays a coffee branch with evergreen leaves,
blossoms and ripe cherries.

The painted interior of St. Benedict's church in Kona, Hawaii.

THE KING AT SOUTH KONA

Face of Hawaii
Islands radiant,
Ridges erect,
Cloud banks seen.

Rising in the sea,
In the whispering sea,
Voice of Ka-wai-hae.
O showers, pour forth.

Old hula lyric, from *Na Mele o Hawai'i Nei: 101 Hawaiian Songs,* 1970, collected by Samuel H. Elbert and Noelani Mahoe

and the damp rich volcanic soil. Many of the best Kona coffees are sold and enjoyed locally on the island—unlike other coffee-growing countries, who export all their best coffees.

A wonderful time to visit Kona's plantations is early to mid-November, when the weather remains beautiful but the summertime tourist crowds have diminished. The harvest is at its peak then, and the area's more than nine hundred growers celebrate with a week-long Kona Coffee Cultural Festival. Such events as a coffee-picking competition, art exhibitions, a grand parade, organized tours of farms and mills, and the Miss Kona Coffee Pageant fill the streets of Kailua and surrounding areas with the enduring spirit of Kona coffee. A particular highlight is the cup-testing to select the year's best beans—a contest in which I've been honored to be a judge on several occasions. It has helped me to learn the true potential of Kona coffee. This is the only event I know of in the world in which coffee growers willingly compete to be named the very best, a tradition that typifies the competitive and independent spirit of the United States.

How the Sun Was Snared ☼

Long ago, so ancient Hawaiian legend tells it, the Sun sped through the sky so quickly that farmers never had enough time to work their crops, and the plants took many years to bear fruit.

The demigod Maui decided to do something about it. He wove sixteen of the strongest ropes ever made, one for each of the Sun's sixteen legs. One night, he snuck into the crater of Haleakala and hid himself in a hole at the base of a wili-wili tree. Come morning, the Sun slowly appeared over the crater's rim, and one by one Maui caught his legs, tying them fast to the tree.

The Sun begged for his release, and he and Maui struck a bargain. For six months of each year, the Sun would move slowly, bringing summer to the islands and allowing the crops to grow. Each winter, the Sun would be allowed to travel more swiftly, so that mankind and the land could rest from their toils.

Participants march to the beat of ancient Japanese taiko drums in the
Kona Coffee Cultural Festival Lantern Parade.

A NOTE ON DECAFFEINATION

Those who desire to linger over their coffee on a summer's evening may well wish to avoid caffeine. That's now easy to accomplish, thanks to decaffeinated versions of such classics as the Gazebo® and House® blends. At Starbucks, the same premium beans chosen for regular varietal coffees are decaffeinated using the gentlest, safest, most advanced processes available. Then they are roasted to develop the same great flavor characteristics you enjoy in their caffeinated versions. So there is no reason to deprive yourself of great coffee at any time of day or night.

Pleasures of Blending

For some people, a visit to one favorite place constitutes the ideal summer vacation. Others, however, prefer to tour several spots in the course of a journey that highlights all their interests. You could say the same thing of blended coffees. Joining together two or more different kinds of coffee beans offers the chance to explore all the characteristics you like in a single cup—or to compose a brew specially suited to the season. At Starbucks, our blends are specially created to capture a very specific flavor experience, a true coffee gestalt, in which the whole is always greater than the sum of its parts. These intricately designed taste experiences bring you all the best each coffee has to offer.

Our House Blend® combines the best of Central and South America to create a balanced and lively cup. This blend is a great introduction to the Starbucks lineup as well as a much-loved favorite of millions of regular customers who frequent our stores each year. Starbucks Gazebo Blend® takes you on a tour of the coffee-growing regions of East Africa and Arabia—places like Kenya, Ethiopia, Malawi, Burundi, Tanzania, Zambia, Zimbabwe and Yemen—to capture the complex berry and fruit flavors that only the best East African coffees offer. Though it is great hot for breakfast, all of its complexity and elegance are enhanced by icing. It becomes loquacious and very refreshing. Versatile, resilient and intricate, this coffee is composed very carefully each year to give summer pleasure to coffee connoisseurs.

Summertime Brewing

Whether you drink your coffee hot or cold in summer usually depends upon the time of day. Most people prefer hot coffee in the morning and evening, and think of iced coffee as the perfect beverage for a sunny afternoon. Some enjoy sipping an iced drink all day long, however, others claim they find hot coffee refreshing when the day heats up. In other words, how you like your coffee is a question of personal taste.

Which coffee you brew poses a question of taste as well. Although the varietals and blends discussed on the previous pages recommend coffees that are, I feel, ideal for summer, a greater truth prevails: Any coffee you like is the right choice.

There is, however, one point on which all coffee lovers agree, especially in summer: They want their coffee fast, with no long waits in a hot kitchen and no lag time between brewing and icing. The instructions that follow will help you get cup or glass to lip as quickly as possible.

For those of you who have never tried iced coffee, live dangerously! Try it this summer. You'll be surprised to taste your favorite brew come alive over ice.

BREWING HOT COFFEE

Four fundamentals stand behind the brewing of every good cup of coffee: proportion, grind, water and freshness. These four principles are important regardless of the following brewing methods you use.

* Proportion, the most critical of them, calls for 2 tablespoons of ground coffee for every 6 ounces of water (or, for espresso, about 1½ tablespoons for a 1- to 1¼-ounce single shot). A plastic scoop (sold in Starbucks stores), delivers that precise amount for the perfect proportion.

* Grind, which refers to how finely or coarsely the coffee is ground, determines how slowly or quickly water will pass through it and, as a result, how much flavor will be extracted. A blade or burr grinder will help achieve the correct grind for the brewing method you use.

* Water should be free of any taste that might affect the coffee's flavor. Use good tap water or filtered or bottled water, heated to just off the boil—195° to 205°F—to extract the right amount of flavor from ground coffee.

* Freshness applies to every stage of coffee brewing. Buy freshly roasted beans from a reputable roaster or retailer; store them away from air, heat, light and moisture; grind them just before brewing and use them within two weeks of purchase. Brew your coffee fresh every time for the best flavor. If necessary, keep it on a warmer for no more than 20 minutes or, better still, put it in a thermal bottle. Never reheat it.

THE PRESS

A traditional French-style coffeemaker, the press yields a rich, flavorful brew with a fine sediment that makes the drink feel satisfyingly thick and full-bodied in the mouth.

* Wash the pot and plunger assembly with hot, soapy water, then rinse both with hot water to preheat.

* Measure into the pot 2 tablespoons of coarsely ground coffee for each 6 ounces of water.

* Add water just off the boil. Stir to mix. Place plunger assembly on top and let steep for 4 minutes.

A HOT, COOLING DRINK

*T*he Turks have a drink of black color, which during the summer is very cooling, whereas in the winter it heats and warms the body, remaining always the same beverage and not changing its substance.

Pietro Della Valle (1586–1652), in a letter from Constantinople dated 1615 to his friend Mario Schipano in Venice, Italy

★ Pointing the spout away and holding the handle securely, slowly press down on the plunger to force the grounds to the bottom. Serve immediately.

THE DRIP FILTER
This popular brewing method uses a cone-shaped or flat-bottomed filter to hold ground coffee in a plastic or pottery basket set on top of a serving pot, thermal bottle, cup or mug. It yields a clean-tasting, full-flavored brew.

* For automatic drip, fill the reservoir with cold, fresh water; for manual, bring water to a boil in a kettle.

* Place a paper filter or a gold-plated permanent filter in the filter basket. Measure in 2 tablespoons of coffee for each 6 ounces of water, using fine grind for cone-shaped filters and medium grind for most flat-bottomed filters.

* For automatic drip, turn on the coffeemaker; for manual, slowly pour the right amount water, just off the boil, over the ground coffee.

* When all of the water has dripped through, briefly stir the coffee, then serve immediately.

THE ESPRESSO MACHINE

Designed to force hot water at high pressure through very finely ground—but not powdery—coffee, these machines, which are now widely available in home models, produce a few sips of nectarlike coffee crowned with a soft, golden froth.

* Fill the machine's reservoir with cold, fresh water.
* Plug in the machine.
* Fill the filter basket to the rim with espresso-grind coffee: approximately 1 ½ tablespoons for a single-shot, full-sized filter insert. Tamp down lightly but evenly. Clamp the filter securely into the machine and place the cup underneath.
* When the water is ready, flip the switch, push the button or pull the lever to start forcing the hot water through coffee.
* Turn off the machine after about 20 seconds, when you have 1 to 1¼ ounces for a single shot or 2 ounces for a double shot from a large filter. Serve immediately.

MAKING ICED COFFEE

Drinking iced coffee holds many pleasures: the sight of sparkling brown liquid in a tall glass dripping with condensation; a familiar warm aroma suddenly transformed into something crisp and breezy; a long, cool sip, revealing favorite flavors in a refreshing new way. As a general rule, any coffee that tastes good to you hot will taste good iced. I have found, however, that the most delicate-tasting varietals, especially Kona, may be numbed by icing. Coffees with rich flavor, such as Ethiopia Sidamo, or with the bright acidity found in Kenyan beans, retain their character over ice. And some, like Starbucks Gazebo Blend®, actually achieve their fullest potential when iced.

Whichever coffee you choose to chill, keep in mind that ice cubes will dilute its full flavor if brewed in the usual way. To prevent this from happening, follow these simple steps:

* Using twice the usual proportion of coffee to water, brew double-strength fresh, hot coffee with a drip filter or, preferably, a press (pages 36–37).
* Fill a pitcher completely with ice cubes. The pitcher should hold about twice the volume of coffee you are brewing.
* As soon as the coffee is brewed, pour it hot directly over the ice cubes. They will partially melt as they chill the coffee, diluting it to the proper strength.

COFFEE ICE CUBES

If you have leftover coffee from brewing a potful, pour it into an ice-cube tray and freeze. Transfer the coffee ice cubes to a freezer bag, and use them to chill regular-strength coffee.

ICED COFFEE ALTERNATIVES

Pouring double-strength coffee over ice cubes is not the only way to make iced coffee. Another method will yield good results as well. **Cold-Water Concentrate**: Widely available cold-water coffeemakers, usually marketed under the Toddy brand name, produce a low-acid liquid concentrate by steeping coarsely ground coffee in cold, fresh water for up to twenty-four hours. The resulting concentrate is filtered and then used to make iced coffee as well as hot coffee. To make iced coffee, add 2 ounces of the concentrate to every 6 ounces of cold, fresh water, and then pour over ice cubes.

Summer Coffee Drinks

As the following recipes so temptingly demonstrate, iced coffee is only the beginning of summertime coffee pleasures. Combined with milk or cream, chocolate or other flavorings, and poured over ice or whirled into a frosty slush, freshly brewed coffee or espresso is transformed into a wide range of memorable drinks. Use your favorite brand of coffee- or espresso-flavored ice cream in the recipes that call for it.

Shaken Espresso

2 shots double-strength freshly brewed espresso

½ cup half-and-half or heavy cream

2 teaspoons superfine sugar or almond -or hazelnut - flavored syrup

crushed ice

☀ In a small pitcher, stir together the espresso, half-and-half and sugar until well blended. Fill 2 tall glasses with crushed ice and divide the espresso mixture evenly between them. Cover and shake well before serving.
Serves 2

Mocha Slush

6 cups double-strength freshly brewed dark roast coffee

⅔ cup unsweetened cocoa powder, plus additional cocoa powder for garnish

2 cups nonfat milk

☀ Fill ice-cube trays with half of the brewed coffee and place in the freezer. In a bowl, combine the remaining brewed coffee, the ⅔ cup cocoa powder and milk and stir to dissolve the cocoa. Cover and chill.
☀ When the ice cubes have frozen, transfer them to a kitchen towel and, using a hammer or mallet, crush the cubes.
☀ To serve, fill 4 tall glasses with the crushed ice and divide the coffee-cocoa mixture evenly among them. Dust the top with cocoa powder, if using, and serve.
Serves 4

Java Float and Shaken Espresso

Java Float

4 tablespoons chocolate
  syrup

2 cups club soda or sparkling water, chilled

4 scoops coffee ice cream

☀ In each of 2 tall glasses, stir together 2 tablespoons of the chocolate syrup and 1 cup of the club soda. Place 2 scoops of the ice cream in each glass and serve at once.
Serves 2

Borgia Cappuccino and Mocha Slush

Borgia Cappuccino

3 ounces bittersweet chocolate

4 cups milk

4 cinnamon sticks, each about 2 inches long, broken into small pieces

2 tablespoons granulated sugar

1 tablespoon orange extract

¾ cup heavy cream, chilled

ice cubes

zest of 1 orange

☀ In a heavy-bottomed saucepan over low heat, melt the chocolate. Slowly add the milk and then the cinnamon and the sugar, stirring constantly until heated through and well blended. Remove from the heat, cover and chill.

☀ While the chocolate mixture is chilling, in a bowl, combine the orange extract and cream and beat until soft peaks form. Cover and chill.

☀ To serve, fill 4 glasses with ice. Divide the chilled chocolate mixture evenly among them and top each with an equal amount of the whipped cream. Garnish with the orange zest and serve.

Serves 4

Iced Latte

ice cubes

2 shots double-strength
freshly brewed espresso

4 cups cold milk

ground cinnamon or un-
sweetened cocoa powder
(optional)

☀ Fill 2 tall glasses with ice cubes and pour half of the brewed espresso into each glass. Add 2 cups of the milk to each glass, dust the tops with cinnamon, if using, and serve.
Serves 2

Iced Cappuccino

ice cubes

2¾ cups cold milk

2 shots double-strength
freshly brewed espresso

ground cinnamon or un-
sweetened cocoa powder

☀ Fill 2 tall glasses with ice cubes. Pour three quarters of the milk into a pitcher and foam it, using the espresso machine's steam jet. Pour half of the brewed espresso into each glass. Add 1 cup of the remaining milk to each glass. Top evenly with the foamed milk, dust with cinnamon and serve.
Serves 2

Iced Latte and Iced Cappuccino

Summertime Pleasures

☼

On the pages that follow, we present six menus inspired
by summertime pleasures and the coffees that go with
them: a mountain campfire, a backyard brunch, a hiking trailside lunch, a picnic at the beach, an afternoon
by the pool and a boating trip at sunset. Any one of the
recipes can be prepared on its own as a snack to enjoy
with coffee; two or more dishes will create a more elaborate meal that will enhance the occasion even more.

     These recipes were created primarily for kitchen
use; however, if you plan to assemble your meal outdoors while pursuing any of the suggested activities,
there are tips and ideas for packing, on-site prepara-
tion and food storage in each recipe head note. One
word of caution for any ingredients you plan to carry
out with you: Always leave perishables refrigerated until
the last possible minute, then tuck them into insulated
containers with cold packs and do not leave them out
for any length of time.

     You'll also discover, scattered throughout these
pages, helpful sidebars, serving suggestions, and some
of our favorite literary musings to encourage you to
bask in the many pleasures summertime has to offer.

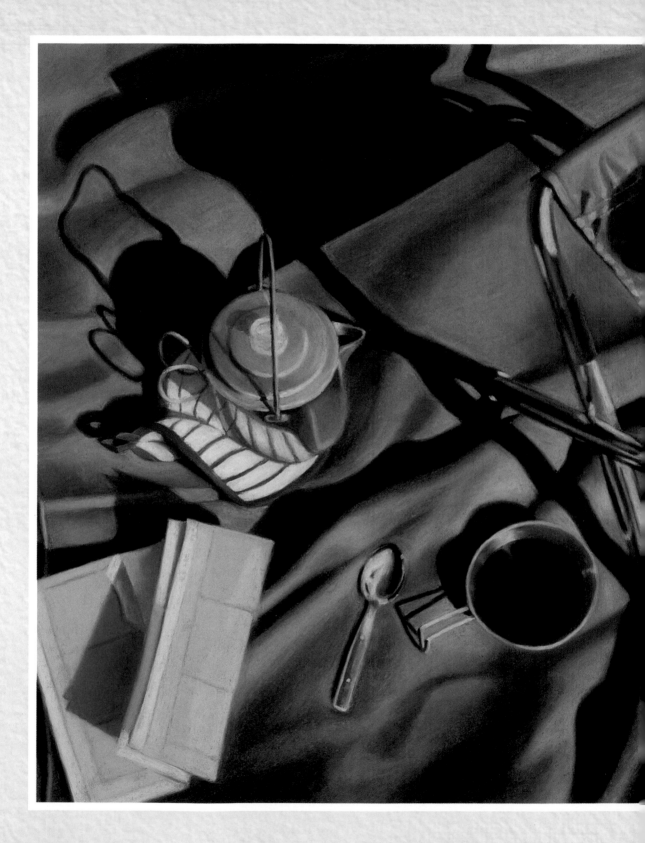

Mountain Campfire Breakfast

Even at the height of summer, there's usually a crisp bite to the morning air when you're camping in the mountains. A campfire chases that chill away and provides the perfect means to cook an outdoor breakfast.

The recipes you'll find on the next few pages are hearty morning fare, offering a range of options for starting the day—whether you've just crawled out of a sleeping bag at a campsite or rolled out from beneath an eiderdown in a mountain cabin. Truth be told, these recipes add their own rustic satisfaction to any morning.

Go for a straightforward, robust coffee selection to accompany your breakfast, such as Kenya or Starbucks House Blend®. If you like, brew them the old-fashioned campfire way (page 48).

Morning Bruschetta

⅓ cup unsalted butter, melted and cooled

½ cup granulated sugar

½ teaspoon ground cinnamon

8 slices firm-textured crusty bread, or 8 slices pound cake, each about 1 inch thick

Nutella hazelnut spread for serving

If you don't have a grill, toast the bread for the bruschetta by spearing each slice with a skewer (as you would a marshmallow) and holding it over the open fire. Nutella, a popular French chocolate spread can be found in specialty food stores.

To make coffee over a campfire the old-fashioned way, the only equipment you need is a pot or kettle in which to boil the water, a jug large enough to hold as much as you might want to brew and a small, fine-mesh metal strainer. Follow these simple steps:

* *Pack the coffee.* In a lock-top plastic bag, pack coffee freshly ground to a coarse grind.

* *Boil the water.* For each cup you wish to brew, bring 6 ounces of fresh cold water to a boil over the campfire.

* *Brew the coffee.* When the water boils, remove it from the campfire. Place in the jug 2 tablespoons of ground coffee for every 6 ounces of water, then pour the hot water over the coffee. Stir with a spoon and let steep for 4 minutes.

* *Strain the coffee.* Holding the strainer over each mug, pour the coffee through the strainer.

☀ Preheat a broiler, place a grill over the campfire, or preheat an oven to 500°F.

☀ In a small bowl, stir together the melted butter, sugar and cinnamon. Set aside.

☀ Toast the slices of bread. Spread each slice on one side with 1 tablespoon of the sugar mixture. Place on a baking sheet, topping side up. Place under the broiler or in the oven until the topping melts and bubbles, about 1 minute under the broiler or 4–5 minutes in the oven.

☀ Remove from the broiler or oven and let cool for 2–3 minutes. Serve the bruschetta warm. Pass the Nutella.

Serves 8

Fruit Kabobs
with Yogurt-Orange Dipping Sauce

For the Dipping Sauce:

2 cups plain yogurt

½ cup confectioners' sugar

2 tablespoons grated orange zest

½ teaspoon vanilla extract

For the Fruit Kabobs:

20 cubes fresh pineapple (1-inch cubes; about 2 cups total)

20 cubes cantaloupe (1-inch cubes; about 2 cups total)

20 cubes honeydew melon (1-inch cubes; about 2 cups total)

20 whole strawberries, stemmed

20 red seedless grapes (about ¾ cup total)

20 green seedless grapes (about ¾ cup total)

Vary fruits with the season. The dipping sauce and fruit cubes can be made ahead. Toss the fruits in lemon juice to prevent discoloration and store in an airtight container, assemble them at campsite.

☀ To make the dipping sauce, in a bowl, stir together the yogurt, confectioners' sugar, orange zest and vanilla extract until smooth. Cover and refrigerate until serving.

☀ To assemble the kabobs, thread the prepared fruits, alternating them, onto eight 10-inch bamboo skewers. Lay the filled skewers on a platter.

☀ Serve the kabobs accompanied with the dipping sauce.

Serves 8

They came back to camp wonderfully refreshed, glad-hearted, and ravenous; and they soon had the campfire blazing up again. Huck found a spring of clear cold water close by, and the boys made cups of broad oak or hickory leaves, and felt that water, sweetened with such a wild-wood charm as that, would be a good substitute for coffee.

Mark Twain, *The Adventures of Tom Sawyer*, 1876

Breakfast Burritos

12 eggs

1½ teaspoons salt

½ teaspoon freshly ground pepper

¼ cup unsalted butter

1½ cups chopped green onions

3 cups refried beans, heated

8 flour tortillas, each 10 inches in diameter, warmed

2 cups shredded Monterey Jack or Cheddar cheese

1 cup salsa

½ cup chopped fresh cilantro (optional)

sour cream or plain yogurt and additional salsa for serving

Warm the tortillas and beans while the egg mixture cooks, or wrap each assembled burrito in aluminum foil and warm on the grill.

☀ In a bowl, beat the eggs with the salt and pepper. In a large skillet (preferably nonstick) over medium-low heat, melt the butter. Add the onion and sauté for 2 minutes. Add the eggs and cook, stirring almost constantly, until done, 7–10 minutes for softly scrambled eggs. Remove from the heat.
☀ To assemble the burritos, spread about ⅓ cup refried beans down the center of each warmed tortilla. Spoon about ⅓ cup of the scrambled eggs over and alongside the beans, and then sprinkle with about ¼ cup cheese. Top with 2 tablespoons of salsa and a sprinkling of cilantro, if using. Fold the sides of the tortilla over the filling, then tuck in one of the ends; leave the other end open.
☀ Place the burritos on individual plates and serve at once. Pass the sour cream and additional salsa.
Serves 8

Twice-Baked Potatoes

4 large baking potatoes, 8–10 ounces each

½ cup milk or heavy cream

¼ cup unsalted butter

1 teaspoon salt

½ teaspoon freshly ground pepper

pinch of ground nutmeg

2 tablespoons chopped fresh parsley

1 cup shredded Gruyère or Swiss cheese

For an easy campfire version, wrap each potato in aluminum foil and bury in campfire coals to bake, then proceed as directed.

☀ Preheat an oven to 450°F.
☀ Prick each potato several times with a fork. Bake on the oven rack until the skin is crackly and the inside is soft when pierced with a knife, 60–70 minutes. Remove from the oven and set aside. Reduce the oven temperature to 400°F.
☀ When the potatoes are cool enough to handle, cut them in half lengthwise. Using a spoon, scoop the pulp into a large bowl, leaving the skin and a ¼-inch-thick shell intact. Set the hollowed-out potato halves aside.
☀ To the pulp, add the milk, butter, salt, pepper and nutmeg. Mash until smooth with a fork or potato masher. Stir in the parsley and ¾ cup of the cheese until well mixed. Spoon the mixture into the potato shells. Top each potato with an equal amount of the remaining cheese and place on a baking sheet.
☀ Bake until the filling is puffy and browned, 25–30 minutes.
☀ Remove from the oven and serve immediately.
Serves 8

Breakfast Burrito and Twice-Baked Potato

Biscuit Breakfast Sandwiches

For the Biscuits:

3 cups all-purpose flour

1 tablespoon baking powder

2 tablespoons granulated sugar

1 teaspoon baking soda

1 teaspoon salt

⅔ cup unsalted butter, at room temperature

1 cup buttermilk

16 slices Cheddar cheese, each 3 inches in diameter and ⅛ inch thick

8 slices cooked ham, each 3 inches in diameter and ¼ inch thick

8 slices tomato, each 3 inches in diameter and ¼ inch thick

For a camping trip bake the biscuits in advance. Store them in an airtight container or bag and assemble the sandwiches at the campsite. Wrap each sandwich in aluminum foil and bury it in the coals of the campfire until the cheese melts and the sandwich is heated through, about 10 minutes.

☀ Preheat oven to 425°F. Line a baking sheet with aluminum foil.

☀ To make the biscuits, in a bowl, sift together the flour, baking powder, sugar, baking soda and salt. Add the butter and, using floured fingertips, work it in until crumbly. Add the buttermilk and stir until a cohesive mass forms.

☀ Place on a floured work surface and knead gently 10 times. Pat into a rectangle about ½ inch thick. Using a biscuit cutter 3 inches in diameter, cut out as many biscuits as possible. Gather up the dough scraps, press them together, pat out again ½ inch thick and cut out more biscuits. You will need 8 biscuits in all.

☀ Place the biscuits on the prepared baking sheet. Bake until golden, 15–18 minutes. Remove from the oven and let cool. Leave the oven set at 425°F.

☀ Split the biscuits in half horizontally, leaving the bottom halves on the baking sheet. Place on each bottom a slice of cheese, a slice of ham, a slice of tomato and then another slice of cheese. Set the biscuit tops in place.

☀ Drape a sheet of aluminum foil loosely over the sandwiches and bake until the cheese melts, 8–10 minutes. Remove from the oven and serve.

Serves 8

Biscuit Breakfast Sandwiches

Backyard Brunch

When the sun shines on a weekend morning, you need go no farther than your own backyard—or a terrace, balcony or large window—to enjoy the pleasures of summer. A favorite deck chair, a table shaded by an umbrella, perhaps the Sunday paper or the company of a few good friends are all you need to make the morning complete.

Except, of course, you will need food and coffee. The recipes that follow are tailored to be savored late on a weekend morning, combining as they do everyday breakfast foods with more filling fare. Any one of them will make a sunny morning special; combine two or more recipes to compose a brunch menu for entertaining.

To drink along with them, select and brew a favorite coffee—aromatic, smooth and bright Ethiopia Sidamo or Yergacheffe, or complex and elegant Starbucks Gazebo Blend®. Brew fresh coffee using your favorite brewing method and keep coffee hot in an attractive thermos that can be poured directly at table all morning long.

Goat Cheese and Sun-Dried Tomato Stratta

Serve this brunch appetizer on crackers, toasted bread or savory scones (see recipe below).

½ cup unsalted butter, at room temperature

¼ pound cream cheese, at room temperature

10 ounces fresh goat cheese, at room temperature

½ teaspoon salt

¼ teaspoon freshly ground pepper

½ cup drained oil-packed sun-dried tomatoes, chopped

1 cup pesto, homemade or purchased

fresh basil or parsley sprigs

❈ Rinse a double-thick 12-inch square of cheesecloth with water and wring damp-dry. Spread the cloth in the interior of a 3- or 4-cup, straight-sided mold (a small bread pan or bowl will work well), letting the excess hang over the rim.

❈ In a food processor, combine the butter, cream cheese, goat cheese, salt and pepper. Process until smooth. Add the tomatoes and process just until finely chopped.

❈ Spread one-third of the cheese mixture across the prepared mold, then bang the mold to settle the contents. Top with half of the pesto, and then with half of the remaining cheese mixture. Again bang the mold. Spread the remaining pesto on top, and then the remaining cheese mixture; bang the mold again. Cover and chill for at least 4 hours.

❈ To serve, invert a serving platter on top of the mold. Then, holding them together, invert the mold. Lift off the mold and peel off the cheesecloth. Garnish with basil or parsley.

Makes about 4 cups; serves 8–12

Savory Scones

8 tablespoons unsalted butter

½ cup thinly sliced green onions

2 tablespoons chopped fresh thyme

2½ cups all-purpose flour

1 tablespoon baking powder

2 teaspoons granulated sugar

1 teaspoon salt

¼ teaspoon freshly ground pepper

⅔ cup milk

1 egg, lightly beaten

1 tablespoon heavy cream

❈ Preheat an oven to 425°F.

❈ In a small skillet over medium heat melt 2 tablespoons of the butter. Add the green onions and sauté until wilted, about 3 minutes. Stir in the thyme and set aside.

❈ In a large bowl, sift together the flour, baking powder, sugar, salt and pepper. Add the remaining 6 tablespoons butter and, using your fingertips, work in the butter until crumbly. Add the milk, egg and the onion mixture and, using a fork, stir just until moistened. The dough will be soft.

❈ Place on a well-floured work surface. Knead gently about 10 times. Divide in half and pat each half into a round about 7 inches in diameter. Brush the tops evenly with the cream, and then cut each round into 6 pie-shaped wedges.

❈ Using a spatula, transfer the rounds to an ungreased baking sheet. Bake until puffy and browned, 15–18 minutes. Remove from the oven and transfer to a rack and serve warm.

Makes 12 scones

Goat Cheese and Sun-Dried Tomato Strata and Savory Scones

Croque-Monsieur

12 slices firm-textured white
    sandwich bread

12 teaspoons unsalted
    butter, at room
    temperature

12 thin slices Gruyère
    cheese, the same size as
    the bread

6 thin slices cooked ham, the
    same size as the bread

⅓–½ cup clarified butter

This French variation on the beloved grilled cheese sandwich uses intensely flavored Gruyère cheese, making it a delicious addition to any brunch menu. For a heartier sandwich, try a croque-madame, which tops the same sandwich with an egg.

When entertaining in your garden or on your patio, terrace or balcony, think of it as an outdoor room. Although the mood may be casual, pay as much attention to setting a scene as you would if you were serving brunch indoors:

* *Keep it colorful.* Cover the table with a bright cloth or place mats, and use complementary napkins.

* *Decorate with an outdoor theme.* Add simple decorations that reflect the outdoor setting or the season, such as informally arranged flowers from the garden or an edible centerpiece of fresh fruits.

☀ Spread each slice of bread on one side with 1 teaspoon butter. Cover 6 of the slices with a slice of Gruyère cheese. Top with a slice of ham and then another slice of cheese and the remaining bread, buttered side down. Press each sandwich together firmly with your palm. Using a long, sharp knife, trim off the crusts.

☀ Add enough clarified butter to a large skillet to form a film on the bottom and place over medium heat. Add as many sandwiches as will fit comfortably in a single layer and cook, turning once, until the bread is golden and the cheese melts, 2–3 minutes on each side. Transfer to a cutting board and keep warm. Add more clarified butter as needed to the pan and cook the remaining sandwiches in the same manner.

☀ To serve, cut the sandwiches into quarters.
Serves 6–8

Torta Rustica

1 box (17¼ ounces) frozen
    puff pastry, in 2 sheets

3 tablespoons olive oil

1 onion, finely chopped

½ pound fresh mushrooms,
    sliced

2 packages (10 ounces each)
    frozen chopped spinach,
    thawed and squeezed
    to remove excess liquid

4 eggs, lightly beaten

2 cup diced, cooked ham

1 teaspoon salt

½ teaspoon freshly ground
    pepper

pinch of nutmeg

6 tablespoons heavy cream

½ pound Swiss or provolone
    cheese, sliced

Although this layered savory pie might seem elaborate, it's actually quite easy to assemble—a task made even simpler by using the ready-to-bake puff pastry now widely available in supermarket freezer cases.

☼ Preheat an oven to 375°F. Butter an 8-inch springform pan.
☼ On a floured surface, roll out one of the pastry sheets into a 12-inch square. Transfer to the prepared pan. Chill the other pastry sheet.
☼ In a large skillet, warm the olive oil. Add the onion and mushrooms and sauté for 5 minutes. Add the spinach and cook until tender, about 5 more minutes. Set aside.
☼ Add the eggs, ham, salt, pepper, nutmeg and 4 tablespoons of the cream to the spinach mixture and stir to mix well. In this order, layer the ingredients in the pastry-lined pan: one third of the spinach mixture, half of the sliced cheese, half of the remaining spinach mixture, the remaining cheese and the remaining spinach mixture. Brush the pastry edge with some of the remaining cream. Cut the second pastry sheet into a 9-inch round and place it over the filling. Press the edges together to seal, then trim the overhanging pastry. Cut 6–8 steam vents on top and brush lightly with cream.
☼ Bake for 15 minutes, then reduce the heat to 350°F. Bake until puffy and browned, 50–60 minutes longer. Transfer to a rack and cool for 1 hour, then remove the pan sides. Serve warm, at room temperature or chilled.
Serves 8

Baked French Toast

2–4 tablespoons unsalted butter, at room temperature

6 eggs

1½ cups milk, half-and-half or heavy cream

3 tablespoons granulated sugar

1 teaspoon vanilla extract

½ teaspoon ground cinnamon

½ teaspoon salt

12 slices brioche or challah, each ¾ to 1 inch thick

confectioners' sugar and maple syrup

This rich-tasting French toast is delicious with a fresh fruit smoothie. Combine 1 cup of milk, 1 cup of plain yogurt and 3 cups of sliced fresh fruit (bananas, figs, strawberries, oranges, etc.) in a blender with a tablespoon of honey and a scoop of crushed ice and blend at high speed until smooth and frothy. Pour into tall glasses and serve at once.

☼ Preheat an oven to 500°F. Grease a large baking sheet or an ovenproof griddle with 2 tablespoons butter.

☼ In a large bowl, using a whisk, beat together the eggs, milk, sugar, vanilla, cinnamon and salt until blended. Pour through a strainer into a large shallow bowl. Dip each bread slice into the egg batter, turning it a few times so that it absorbs the liquid but is not saturated. Set aside.

☼ Heat the prepared pan in the oven for about 3 minutes. Quickly place the bread in a single layer in the hot pan (bake in 2 batches, if necessary). Bake until the bottoms are golden, 5–7 minutes. Flip the bread slices and bake again until bottoms are golden, about 3–5 minutes longer. Do not worry if the butter browns. If you are cooking a second batch, wipe the hot pan with paper towels, grease with 2 more tablespoons butter, and then bake as directed. Transfer the French toast to warmed individual plates and dust with confectioners' sugar. Pass the maple syrup.

Serves 6–8

Peach Shortcakes with Sour Cream

For the Shortcakes:

2½ cups cake flour

⅓ cup granulated sugar

2 teaspoons baking powder

½ teaspoon baking soda

½ teaspoon salt

⅓ cup unsalted butter, at room temperature

1 cup sour cream

For the Fruit and Topping:

8 ripe peaches (3½–4 pounds total), halved, pitted, peeled and sliced

2 tablespoons freshly squeezed lemon juice

2 tablespoons bourbon or brandy

⅓ cup granulated sugar, or to taste, plus 3 tablespoons granulated sugar

1 cup heavy cream

1 teaspoon vanilla extract

½ cup sour cream

A memorable treatment for one of summer's most delicious pleasures. If you like, use other soft fruits, such as nectarines, plums or juicy berries or whatever else is in season.

☀ Preheat an oven to 425°F. To make the shortcakes, in a bowl, sift together the flour, sugar, baking powder, baking soda and salt. Using your fingertips, work in the butter until crumbly. Add the sour cream and stir until a cohesive mass forms.

☀ Place on a well-floured work surface. Knead gently about 10 times. Pat into a rectangle ¾ inch thick. Using a cutter 2½ to 3 inches in diameter, cut out 8 rounds. Place close together on an ungreased baking sheet. Bake until puffy and golden, about 15 minutes. Transfer to a rack to cool.

☀ To prepare the fruit, in a bowl, toss the peaches with the lemon juice, bourbon and the ⅓ cup sugar, set aside.

☀ To make the topping, in a bowl, whip the cream until thickened. Add the vanilla and the 3 tablespoons sugar and whip until stiff. Gently stir in the sour cream.

☀ To serve, split each shortcake horizontally and place the bottoms on individual plates. Spoon about ½ cup fruit over each bottom. Set the tops in place and spoon on remaining fruit. Crown with the topping.

Serves 8

Trailside Lunch

In summer, the open trail beckons with special allure: the crunch of gravel underfoot, the heady scent of sunlight on evergreen, the beauty of nature all around, the satisfying weariness that sets in after a long hike.

Any food you eat along the trail seems well earned. But traveling light, of course, remains the goal, so nothing you carry can be too bulky or heavy. The trailside recipes given here meet the requirements of good hiking provisions: easy to pack, lightweight, flavorful and full of the complex carbohydrates you need for fuel. Any one of them would make a good quick snack; bring along several if you'll be on the trail—or on the road—for a longer stretch of time.

Savory Biscotti

2½ cups all-purpose flour

2 teaspoons baking powder

2 teaspoons coarse (kosher) salt, or 1¼ teaspoons regular salt

½ teaspoon freshly ground pepper

½ cup unsalted butter, at room temperature, cut in 8 pieces

1 cup chopped walnuts

½ cup freshly grated Parmesan cheese

2 eggs

¼ cup milk

¼ cup drained, oil-packed sun-dried tomatoes, finely chopped

2 tablespoons chopped fresh rosemary or 2 teaspoons dried

2 large cloves garlic, minced

Here, the savory flavors of Parmesan cheese, garlic, sun-dried tomatoes and herbs impart a surprising new twist to the crisp, twice-baked cookies of Italy (pictured opposite).

☀ Preheat an oven to 375°F.

☀ In a bowl, sift together the flour, baking powder, salt and pepper. Add the butter and, using fingertips, work it in until crumbly. Add the walnuts and cheese and stir to combine. Set the mixture aside.

☀ In a small bowl, beat together the eggs, milk, tomatoes, rosemary and garlic. Add to the flour mixture and stir vigorously until the dough forms a rough mass.

☀ Transfer to a lightly floured work surface and divide in half. Lightly flour each piece and shape it into a log about 1½ inches in diameter and 10 inches long. Place the logs about 3 inches apart on an ungreased baking sheet. Press down on each until it is about 3 inches wide and ¾ inch high.

☀ Bake until puffed and lightly browned, about 20 minutes. Remove from the oven and let cool 10 minutes on the pan, then slide the logs onto a work surface. Leave the oven set at 375°F.

☀ Using a long, sharp knife, cut each log crosswise into slices ¾ inch thick. Make each cut with a single motion of the blade; do not use a sawing action, or the cookies will break.

☀ Place the cookies, cut side down, on the baking sheet (the cookies can touch). Bake for 10 minutes. Remove from the oven and, using tongs, turn over each cookie. Return to the oven and bake until golden, about 12 minutes longer. Transfer to racks to cool completely. Store in an airtight container.

Makes about 32 biscotti

Santa Fe Trail Mix

½ tablespoon chili powder

1½ teaspoons coarse (kosher) salt

finely grated zest of 2 limes

2 tablespoons walnut oil or olive oil

2½ cups walnuts, in halves or large pieces

1 cup diced, dried pears (about 4 ounces)

½ cup dried currants or dark raisins

Today, nearly everyone is more conscious of the need to take care of the planet's finite resources. Keep these ideas in mind when packing your provisions for the trail:
* *Reduce the number of wrappers.* Try not to wrap too many things individually. If you're hiking with companions, let each person carry a different snack in a single container.
* *Reuse what you have brought.* Pack your snacks in lock-top plastic bags or lightweight airtight containers. After you return home, rinse out and air-dry the bags and containers for reuse.
* *Trash in, trash out.* Bring along a small trash bag that will fit in your backpack, and use it. Don't dispose of anything along the trail.

This familiar trailside snack carries a hint of south-western spice. Feel free to substitute your favorite nuts or dried fruit.

☀ Preheat an oven to 350°F.
☀ In a small cup or bowl, stir together the chili powder, salt and lime zest; set aside.
☀ Spread the walnut oil in a shallow baking pan and set in the oven until the oil is hot, 4–5 minutes. Remove from the oven and add the walnuts. Stir to coat them with the oil. Sprinkle with the chili powder mixture and stir again until combined. Continue to bake, stirring every 5 minutes or so, until the nuts are light brown, about 15 minutes. Remove from the oven and let cool completely.
☀ Add the pears and currants to the nut mixture and toss to combine. Store in an airtight container.
Makes about 4 cups; serves 6–10

½ teaspoon dried thyme or oregano

½ teaspoon salt

¼ teaspoon freshly ground pepper

6–8 Asian eggplants or 1 globe eggplant (1 pound total)

2 baguettes

6 tablespoons bottled black olive paste or sun-dried tomato spread

2 tablespoons drained capers

1 jar (7¼ ounces) roasted red sweet peppers, drained

2 tomatoes, thinly sliced

1 small red onion, thinly sliced and separated into rings

25–30 large fresh basil leaves

½ cup olive oil

2 tablespoons freshly squeezed lime or lemon juice

1 tablespoon sesame oil

1 tablespoon soy sauce

1 large clove garlic, minced

½ teaspoon freshly ground pepper

40–50 asparagus spears (2½–3 pounds total), washed and trimmed

2 tablespoons toasted sesame seeds

Baguette Sandwiches

Baguettes hold up much better than sliced bread when stuffed with sandwich fillings, making them ideal for carrying in a backpack.

☀ Preheat a broiler. In a small bowl, stir together ¼ cup of the olive oil, the thyme, salt and pepper; set aside. Trim off the eggplant stems. Cut the Asian eggplants in half lengthwise, or cut the globe eggplant crosswise into slices ⅜ inch thick. Brush the eggplant pieces on both sides with the oil mixture and arrange on the rack of a broiler pan.

☀ Broil, turning 2 or 3 times, until browned on both sides, about 10 minutes total. Set aside to cool.

☀ Using a sharp knife, split the baguettes in half lengthwise. Using the tines of a fork, scoop out most of the bready interior from each half. Brush each half with 2 tablespoons of the remaining olive oil. Set the tops aside.

☀ Evenly spread both bottom hollows with 3 tablespoons of the olive paste and sprinkle with 1 tablespoon of the capers. Then layer each with half of the red peppers, half of the eggplant, half of the tomato slices, half of the onion rings and half of the basil leaves. Set the tops in place and press down firmly on the sandwiches. Wrap tightly in plastic wrap and refrigerate until needed.

☀ To serve, unwrap and cut each sandwich into 3 or 4 pieces.
Serves 6–8

Asparagus with Sesame Vinaigrette

☀ To make the vinaigrette, in a jar or other container with a secure lid, combine the olive oil, lime juice, sesame oil, soy sauce, garlic and pepper. Cap tightly and shake vigorously to mix. Refrigerate until needed.

☀ Place the asparagus on a steamer rack over boiling water, cover the steamer and steam until the spears droop slightly when lifted and are easily pierced with the point of a sharp knife, 4–8 minutes. The timing depends upon their size.

☀ Remove the asparagus from the steamer and arrange in a single layer on a clean towel. Let cool completely.

☀ To serve, pour the dressing over the asparagus and sprinkle with the sesame seeds.
Serves 6–8

Baguette Sandwiches and Asparagus with Sesame Vinaigrette

For the Coffee:

½ cup ground coffee

4 cups water

For the Cocoa:

1 cup water

⅓ cup unsweetened cocoa
   powder

⅓ cup granulated sugar

pinch of salt

3 cups milk or
   half-and-half

¼ teaspoon vanilla extract

1 cup all-purpose flour

½ teaspoon baking soda

½ teaspoon salt

1 cup quick-cooking rolled
   oats

1 cup shredded coconut

¾ cup firmly packed brown
   sugar

½ cup sunflower seeds

½ cup coarsely chopped
   golden raisins

½ cup unsalted butter, at
   room temperature

2 tablespoons water

6 ounces semisweet
   chocolate, melted
   (optional)

Hot Coffee Cocoa

Coffee and chocolate blended together and kept hot in a thermos make for a soothing drink at the end of the trail.

☀ To make the coffee, brew the measured amounts of coffee and water, using your customary method. Keep the coffee hot.
☀ To make the cocoa, in a saucepan over medium heat, stir together the water, cocoa powder, sugar and salt. Cook, whisking constantly, until the mixture is smooth, then bring just to a boil. Add the milk and return to a simmer. Remove from the heat and stir in the vanilla.
☀ Combine the hot coffee and hot cocoa. Serve in mugs or heat-resistant glasses.
Serves 6–8

Anzac Cookies

Named in honor of the Australian and New Zealand Army Corps, these nutrition-packed cookies are a good energy boost.

☀ Preheat an oven to 350°F. Cover a baking sheet with aluminum foil.
☀ In a large bowl, sift together the flour, baking soda and salt. Add the oats, coconut, brown sugar, sunflower seeds and raisins; stir until combined. Using your fingertips, work the butter in until crumbly. Add the water and stir until a cohesive mass forms.
☀ On a floured work surface, using floured fingers, pat dough into a rectangle ½ inch thick. Using a cookie cutter 2 inches in diameter, cut out rounds. Place 1 inch apart on the prepared baking sheet. Gather up the dough scraps and pat out again ½ inch thick and cut out more cookies.
☀ Bake until golden brown, about 15 minutes. Transfer to racks to cool completely.
☀ To dip the cookies in chocolate, place the melted chocolate in a small bowl. Dip each cookie about one-fourth of the way into the chocolate, to coat partially. Place on a sheet of waxed paper and let stand until the chocolate is firm, about 3 hours. To store, layer between sheets of waxed paper in an airtight container.
Makes about 24 cookies

Hot Coffee Cocoa and Anzac Cookies

Beach Picnic

A day at the beach and all the many pleasures derived from it are, for most people, definitive summertime experiences: bright sunshine, a towel or blanket on the sand, a good book to read or a radio to listen to, a playful splash or a vigorous swim in the surf, and a flavorful picnic to snack on all afternoon long.

The beach picnic recipes on these pages lend themselves well to such idle nibbling, with chicken sandwiches, zesty stuffed and marinated vegetables and rich cookies. The seasonings here take their inspiration from sun-kissed Mediterranean cuisines.

With these dishes, the ideal coffee to sip, whether hot or iced, is Starbucks Gazebo Blend®. Clean and crisp, it provides perfect refreshment from the heat of the beach. Alternatively, try the Iced Constantine Coffee recipe on page 76, which nicely complements this highly seasoned fare.

Mediterranean Antipasto Platter

You'll find influences of the coastal cooking of Italy, France and Spain in these three appealing finger foods. To keep them cold, store in an airtight container in an ice-filled cooler.

For the Stuffed Celery:

¾ pound goat cheese

2 tablespoons sour cream

½ teaspoon salt

⅛ teaspoon freshly ground pepper

¼ cup chopped fresh chives

2 tablespoons chopped fresh tarragon

8–10 tender celery stalks

STUFFED CELERY:

☀ To make the stuffed celery, in a food processor, combine the goat cheese, sour cream, salt and pepper. Process until smooth. Add the chives and tarragon and process until combined. Spread about 3 tablespoons of the mixture in each celery stalk. Cover and chill until the cheese is firm, then cut each stalk into 3-inch long pieces, about 30 pieces total.
Serves 8

For the Stuffed Endive:

¼ pound blue cheese

¼ pound cream cheese

1 tablespoon heavy cream or milk

¼ cup finely chopped, pitted dates

¼ cup finely chopped walnuts, toasted

about 30 large Belgian endive leaves

STUFFED ENDIVE:

☀ To make the stuffed endive, in a food processor, combine the blue cheese, cream cheese and cream. Process until smooth. Add the dates and walnuts and process until combined. Mound about 1½ teaspoons of the cheese mixture on the large end of each endive leaf. Cover and chill until serving.
Serves 8

For the Carrot Sticks:

12–14 carrots (about 2 pounds total), peeled

1½ cups water

¾ cup dry white wine

½ cup olive oil

½ cup white wine vinegar

1 tablespoon chopped fresh thyme or 1 teaspoon dried

1½ teaspoons salt

4 cloves garlic, crushed

1 bay leaf

watercress or fresh parsley for garnish

Pack a beach picnic following these guidelines:

★ *Use lightweight carriers.*

★ *Choose nonbreakable dishware.* Sturdy reusable plastic dishes, drinking vessels and utensils or recyclable paper, cardboard and plastic are light and eliminate worries over breakage.

★ *Bring a cloth or blanket.* A large tablecloth, blanket or towel, spread just before dining, sets a fresh, clean scene.

★ *Pack food wisely.* Pack everything in airtight plastic or rubber containers or lock-top plastic bags. Place a reusable cold pack (many brands are available) next to perishables, and keep food away from direct sunlight. To avoid soggy sandwiches, pack fillings and breads separately, to be assembled just before eating. Keep coffee, whether hot or iced, in a thermal bottle or carafe.

CARROT STICKS:

☀ To make the carrot sticks, halve the carrots lengthwise (or quarter them if they are large) and cut into 3- or 4-inch sticks (about 50 pieces total). In a large skillet, combine the water, wine, olive oil, vinegar, thyme, salt, garlic and bay leaf. Bring to a boil and add the carrots. Reduce the heat to medium and boil gently until the carrot sticks are barely tender when pierced, 10–12 minutes. Let cool, cover and refrigerate.

☀ To serve, drain the carrots then arrange with the celery and endive leaves on a platter and garnish with watercress.

Serves 8

Curried Chicken Sandwiches with Hummus

The lively flavors of sun-drenched cuisines combine in these pita sandwiches: Middle Eastern hummus, Indian curry powder, and Mexican chipotle chilies in *adobo,* which are smoked jalapeños in a vinegar red sauce sold in cans in Latin American markets and well-stocked food stores.

For the Hummus:

2 cans (15 ounces each) garbanzo beans

1 canned chipotle pepper in *adobo* or 1 canned jalapeño pepper

⅓ cup tahini (sesame-seed paste) or smooth peanut butter

¼ cup freshly squeezed lemon juice

4 cloves garlic, crushed

1 teaspoon salt

⅔ cup olive oil

For the Chicken Salad:

⅔ cup mayonnaise

⅔ cup plain yogurt

⅓ cup slivered almonds, toasted

⅓ cup dried currants

1 tablespoon curry powder

¼ teaspoon freshly ground pepper

1 teaspoon salt

5 cups diced, cooked chicken

8 pita breads

16 leaves lettuce

2–3 large tomatoes, thinly sliced

☀ To make the hummus, drain the garbanzo beans. Drain, stem and seed chipotle pepper. In a food processor, combine the chili pepper, garbanzo beans, tahini, lemon juice, garlic and salt. Purée until smooth. With the machine running, add the olive oil in a slow, steady stream and process for 1 minute.

☀ To make the chicken salad, in a large bowl, whisk together the mayonnaise, yogurt, almonds, currants, curry powder, pepper and salt. Add the chicken and stir to combine.

☀ To assemble the sandwiches, halve pita breads to create 16 pockets, spread about 3 tablespoons hummus in each pita pocket. Tuck in a lettuce leaf and a tomato slice and then fill with about ⅓ cup chicken salad. Serve at once or wrap tightly and refrigerate. Serves 8

Heaven, as conventionally conceived, is a place
so inane, so dull, so useless, so miserable, that
nobody has ever ventured to describe a whole day
in heaven, though plenty of people have described
a day at the seaside.

George Bernard Shaw, preface to *Misalliance*

Curried Chicken Sandwiches with Hummus

Greek Wedding Cookies

1 cup walnuts or almonds, toasted

2¾ cups all-purpose flour

1 teaspoon salt

1 cup unsalted butter, at room temperature

2½ cups confectioners' sugar

2 teaspoons vanilla extract

1 tablespoon grated orange zest

½ cup granulated sugar

These traditional Greek treats are so delicious and easy to make that you won't need the excuse of a festive occasion to bake a batch.

☀ Preheat an oven to 350°F. Line a baking sheet with aluminum foil.

☀ In a food processor or blender, grind the nuts finely but not into a paste. In a small bowl, stir together the ground nuts, flour and salt; set aside.

☀ In a large bowl, combine the butter and 2 cups of the confectioners' sugar and, using a wooden spoon, beat until blended and smooth. Beat in the vanilla and orange zest. Add the nut mixture and beat until thoroughly blended (the dough will be stiff and crumbly).

☀ To make each cookie, scoop up 1 tablespoon of the dough and roll between your palms into a smooth ball. Set aside. Place the granulated sugar and the remaining ½ cup confectioners' sugar in separate, shallow bowls. Roll the balls first in the granulated sugar and then in the confectioners' sugar, coating evenly. Place on the prepared baking sheet.

☀ Bake until the cookies have puffed a little and the tops have cracked slightly, 12–14 minutes. Let cool for a moment, then transfer to a rack and let sit, uncovered, until the sugar coating no longer feels damp, several hours or overnight. Store in an airtight container.

Makes about 50 cookies

Iced Constantine Coffee

⅔ cup ground dark-roast coffee

4 cinnamon sticks, crushed or broken into small pieces

6 cups water

½ teaspoon ground cardamom

⅔ cup honey

ice cubes

half-and-half or milk

☀ Mix together the coffee and cinnamon sticks. Using the coffee-cinnamon mixture and the water, brew coffee by your customary brewing method. Add the cardamom and honey to the hot coffee and stir until the honey dissolves. Cover and chill.

☀ To serve, fill tall glasses with ice cubes. Pour about ⅔ cup chilled coffee into each glass. Pass the half-and-half or milk.

Serves 8

Greek Wedding Cookies and Iced Constantine Coffee

Poolside Afternoon Treats

Spending an afternoon beside the pool is one of summer's most delightfully self-indulgent pleasures. You might swim a few laps or choose to do nothing more strenuous than slap on sunscreen or turn the pages of a book.

Poolside foods should be equally self-indulgent, as exemplified by the recipes for homemade ice cream treats, frozen chocolates and frosty cold beverages that follow.

Coffee? Serve it over ice, of course. Try Kenya or Starbucks Gazebo Blend®, both of which possess the bright, clean, yet complex flavor and aroma for cold summer sipping.

Tropical Fruit Drinks

1 cup granulated sugar

1 cup water

3 large mangoes, 3 papayas, or 10–12 kiwifruits, peeled

¼ cup freshly squeezed lime juice

4 cups still water or carbonated mineral water, chilled

Mango, papaya and kiwifruit are especially good choices, but cantaloupe and honeydew melon will also produce refreshing drinks.

☀ In a small saucepan over high heat, combine the sugar and water. Heat, stirring until the sugar dissolves and the liquid is clear. Let cool, cover and chill before using.

☀ If you are using mangoes, remove the pits; if using papayas, remove the seeds (kiwifruits do not need seeding). Cut the pulp into chunks and place in a blender or food processor. Add the lime juice and purée until smooth; you should have about 2 cups of the fruit purée.

☀ In a large pitcher or bowl, stir together the fruit purée and chilled sugar syrup. Add the chilled water and stir to blend. Serve at once over ice.

Serves 6–8

Iced Tea Spritzers

6 cups water, boiling

8 tea bags or ¼–⅓ cup loose tea, either a black tea such as Darjeeling or Ceylon or an herbal or spiced tea

granulated sugar, if needed

For Each Serving:

ice cubes

about ⅔ cup club soda

lemon slices and/or fresh mint sprigs

granulated sugar, preferably superfine

A sparkling way to enjoy a popular summertime beverage. Choose a highly fragrant black or herbal tea.

☀ In a large bowl, combine the boiling water and the tea bags or loose tea. Stir a few times and let steep for 5–7 minutes. Stir the tea again, then either remove the tea bags or strain out the loose tea through a cheesecloth-lined strainer.

☀ If you wish to sweeten the tea, add granulated sugar to taste and stir to dissolve (½ cup sugar added now will make a mildly sweet spritzer). Cover and refrigerate until thoroughly chilled, at least 2 hours. You will have about 6 cups of tea.

☀ For each serving, fill a tall glass with ice cubes, and then fill about half full with tea. Top with club soda. Garnish with a lemon slice and/or mint sprig, and sweeten to taste with sugar.

Serves 8–10

Iced Tea Spritzers and Tropical Fruit Drinks

Ice Cream Sandwiches
with Homemade Oatmeal Cookies

1½ cups all-purpose flour

4 teaspoons ground cardamom

½ teaspoon salt

½ teaspoon baking soda

1 cup unsalted butter, at room temperature

1 cup brown sugar

1 cup granulated sugar

2 eggs

3 cups quick-cooking rolled oats

1–1½ quarts coffee ice cream

Serving an ice cream or sorbet. For soft ice cream or sorbet, serve immediately after churning. Or place in a covered container in the freezer overnight to harden, then transfer to the refrigerator 30 minutes before serving, to soften slightly for easier scooping. * *Serving a water ice or granita.* Serve as soon as the mixture is sufficiently frozen to be scooped up with a spoon. If made in advance, store in an airtight container in the freezer; then let it soften in the refrigerator for about 30 minutes, and fluff with a fork before scooping and serving.

Homemade oatmeal cookies, so wonderful on their own, make extraordinarily good ice cream sandwiches. Your favorite coffee ice cream is a natural choice, but you can use any flavor you like.

❋ Preheat an oven to 350°F. Coat 1 or 2 baking sheets with nonstick cooking spray.

❋ On a sheet of waxed paper, sift together the flour, cardamom, salt and baking soda. Set aside.

❋ In a large bowl, using a wooden spoon or electric mixer, beat together the butter, brown sugar and ½ cup of the granulated sugar until blended. Beat in the eggs, one at a time. Then add the flour mixture and stir vigorously to combine. Add the oats and mix well.

❋ Put the remaining ½ cup granulated sugar in a bowl. For each cookie, scoop up about 2 tablespoons of the dough, roll between your palms into a smooth ball and then roll in the granulated sugar. Place the balls on the prepared baking sheet(s) about 2 inches apart. Using the bottom of a sturdy drinking glass, flatten each cookie into a disk about 3 inches in diameter (dip the glass in sugar if it sticks).

❋ Bake until lightly browned, 12–14 minutes. Transfer to racks and let cool completely.

❋ For each sandwich, place a ½-cup scoop of ice cream between 2 cookies, bottoms inward. Press together so the ice cream spreads to the edges. Immediately wrap in plastic wrap and place in the freezer until serving.

Makes 10 sandwiches, with about 12 cookies leftover

Ice Cream Sandwiches with Homemade Oatmeal Cookies

Ice Cream Parfait

3 tablespoons unsalted
butter

¾ cup granulated sugar

6 peaches (about 3 pounds
total), halved, pitted,
peeled and thinly sliced

2 tablespoons freshly
squeezed lemon juice

½ teaspoon almond extract

1 cup heavy cream

2 tablespoons confectioners'
sugar

½ teaspoon vanilla extract

½ quart vanilla ice cream

½ cup crushed Almond Roca
or peanut brittle

Fresh mint sprigs (optional)

Fresh, juicy summer fruit laces rich ice cream in this easily assembled yet elegant treat. Use the best-quality vanilla ice cream you can find, and chill 8 parfait or sundae glasses or sturdy wineglasses for serving.

☀ In a large, heavy skillet over medium heat, combine the butter and sugar. Cook until the sugar dissolves and the mixture bubbles, about 5 minutes. Add the peaches and lemon juice and cook, stirring frequently, until the fruit is tender and most of the liquid has evaporated, about 10 minutes. Remove from the heat and stir in the almond extract. Let cool at room temperature, then cover and refrigerate until cold.

☀ In a bowl, combine the cream, confectioners' sugar and vanilla. Beat until stiff.

☀ To assemble the parfaits, fill the chilled glasses with alternating layers of the chilled peaches and the ice cream, using about ½ cup of each per serving. Top each parfait with a spoonful of whipped cream and sprinkle evenly with the Almond Roca or peanut brittle. Garnish with mint, if using, and serve at once.

Serves 8

Frozen Chocolate Truffles

9 ounces semisweet chocolate, finely chopped

3 ounces unsweetened chocolate, finely chopped

2 tablespoons bourbon, brandy, rum or orange-flavored liqueur

2 teaspoons vanilla extract

1 ¼ cups heavy cream

⅓ cup confectioners' sugar, sifted

½ cup unsweetened cocoa powder

You'll be surprised at how easy it is to make these sophisticated confections. They store well and they're fun to eat straight from the freezer.

❋ In a large heat-resistant bowl, combine both chocolates, the bourbon and vanilla and set aside.

❋ In a small saucepan over medium heat, bring the cream to a simmer. Add to the chocolate and, using a wire whisk, stir continuously until the chocolate melts and the mixture is smooth and creamy, about 1–2 minutes. Add the confectioners' sugar and whisk until blended. Cover and refrigerate until firm, at least 3 hours or for as long as overnight.

❋ Spread the cocoa in a shallow bowl.

❋ To form each truffle, using a spoon, scoop up about 1 tablespoon of the chilled chocolate mixture and, using your fingertips, rapidly push it into a rough, roundish ball. When you have formed 6–8 truffles, gently roll them about in the cocoa until evenly coated. Transfer them in a single layer to a freezer-safe plate. Repeat until all the chocolate mixture is used.

❋ Freeze the truffles for about 1 hour, then layer them between sheets of waxed paper in a tightly sealed container. Return the truffles to the freezer until frozen solid and serve directly from the freezer. Or for a softer truffle, store in the refrigerator.

Makes 40–45 truffles

Summer afternoon—summer afternoon; to me those have always been the two most beautiful words in the English language.

Henry James, quoted by Edith Wharton in *A Backward Glance*

Boating Sunset Supper

Whether in a rowboat, sailboat or motorized craft, on a river, lake or ocean, a summer day afloat offers its own particular appeal: the shimmer of sunshine, the steady motion of the water, the clean scent of the outdoors. Add the glorious light of sunset and those pleasures are heightened even further.

It is also a setting that whets the appetite for foods whose fresh taste and pleasant tang match the spirit of the surroundings. The following recipes meet such a profile, featuring dishes inspired by the cooking of Southeast Asia, the Mediterranean and Hawaii. Any one on its own would make an ideal boating snack for midday, afternoon or evening.

The coffee you serve, whether hot or iced, should be just as exotic. An Arabian Mocha Sanani or an Ethiopia Sidamo or Yergacheffe would be a good choice.

Thai Noodle Salad with Sesame-Peanut Dressing

For the Dressing:

½ cup smooth peanut butter

¼ cup freshly squeezed lime juice

3 tablespoons soy sauce

1 teaspoon red pepper flakes

¼ cup Asian sesame oil

8–10 drops hot chili oil

2 tablespoons water, if needed

1 pound dried spaghetti, linguine or other thin pasta

½ cup olive oil

1 cup thinly sliced green onions, including tender green tops

½ cup chopped fresh cilantro or parsley, plus cilantro or parsley sprigs for garnish

2 teaspoons black sesame seeds

Reminiscent of satisfying Asian street food, this salad is also good warm, with the dressing gently heated in a saucepan and tossed with the just-cooked pasta. Serve this dish with iced coffee made with a varietal bean from one of Thailand's coffee-growing neighbors: Estate Java, Sumatra or Sulawesi.

☀ To make the dressing, in a small bowl, whisk together the peanut butter, lime juice and soy sauce until smooth. Stir in the red pepper flakes, sesame oil and hot chili oil. If the dressing seems very thick, whisk in the water. Set aside at room temperature to blend the flavors.

☀ Bring a large pot three-fourths full of salted water to a rolling boil. Add the pasta and cook until *al dente,* about 8–10 minutes or according to package directions. Drain thoroughly and place in a large bowl. Add the olive oil and toss until evenly coated. Let cool to room temperature, tossing frequently to prevent the noodles from sticking together.

☀ To serve, pour the dressing over the noodles and toss to coat evenly. Add the green onions and chopped cilantro and toss again to combine. Mound the noodles in a serving bowl or spread out on a large platter. Garnish with sprigs of cilantro and black sesame seeds and serve.

Serves 6–8

Thai Noodle Salad with Sesame-Peanut Dressing

Rolled Lavosh Sandwiches with Smoked Salmon

2 rounds of lavosh (Arme-
nian cracker bread), each
12 inches in diameter

½ pound cream cheese, at
room temperature

½ pound sliced, smoked
salmon

3 tablespoons freshly
squeezed lemon juice

2 tablespoons vodka

¼ teaspoon hot-pepper
sauce

salt, if needed

¼ cup chopped fresh dill or
1 teaspoon dried

1 large red onion, very thinly
sliced

1 large English (hothouse)
cucumber, very thinly
sliced

You'll find lavosh in Middle
Eastern markets, health-
food shops and well-stocked
food stores. If unavailable,
substitute pita breads, split
in two along their edges.

Pack your drinks in a thermal
bottle or carafe. It can keep
beverages steaming hot or icy cold
for many hours. Consider these
points when shopping for one:
* *Size.* Capacity can vary from a
few cups to about ten. A larger
container will be heavier to carry.
* *Shape.* Straight-sided bottles
pack more neatly. Look for
containers that pour without
removing the lid, maintaining the
temperature of the coffee longer.
* *Material.* Outer surfaces may
be plastic or steel; inner thermal
liners may be glass or stainless
steel. Although stainless is
unbreakable, it is not as lightweight as glass or plastic.

☀ Dampen the rounds of lavosh under a gentle stream of cold
running water for about 30 seconds on each side. Place the
rounds close together, but not touching, on a clean, damp
kitchen towel, then cover with a second damp towel.

☀ In a food processor, combine the cream cheese, smoked
salmon, lemon juice, vodka and hot-pepper sauce and process
until smooth. Season with salt, if necessary. Add the dill and
process briefly to blend.

☀ Carefully remove the lavosh from the towels and place the
rounds on a flat work surface. Coat each round with half of the
salmon mixture, spreading it to the edge. Scatter the onion over
the top and then the cucumber slices, dividing them evenly
between the rounds. Roll up each round snugly, as if it were a
carpet. Wrap the rolls in plastic wrap and refrigerate for at least
3 hours or for up to 2 days.

☀ To serve, unwrap the rolls and, using a sharp knife, trim off the
ragged ends. Then cut the rolls crosswise into 1-inch-wide slices
and arrange on a serving platter. Cover with plastic wrap and
refrigerate until serving.

Serves 8–10

Gazpacho of Grilled Summer Vegetables

2 bell peppers, 1 red and
1 green, both seeded
and sliced crosswise into
½-inch-wide rings

1 large red onion, sliced
½ inch thick

2 medium zucchinis, halved
lengthwise

extra-virgin olive oil for
brushing vegetables, plus
⅓ cup olive oil

salt to taste, plus
1 teaspoon salt

freshly ground pepper to
taste, plus ¼ teaspoon
freshly ground pepper

2 pounds ripe tomatoes
(5 or 6), peeled, halved,
seeded and diced

1 English (hothouse)
cucumber, halved, seeded
and diced

3 cups tomato juice

¼ cup white wine vinegar

3 large cloves garlic, minced

hot-pepper sauce

Grilled vegetables have a particularly sweet, more intense flavor, resulting in a memorable variation on Spain's familiar chilled soup. This soup can be transported in a thermos or other nonreactive, spillproof container to enjoy on board.

❋ Prepare a fire in a charcoal grill. Place the bell pepper rings, onion slices and squash halves on a large platter and brush them generously with olive oil. Sprinkle to taste with salt and pepper.
❋ When the coals are ready, place the vegetables on the grill rack and grill, turning them 2 or 3 times, until browned and tender but not mushy, about 5–7 minutes on each side. Remove the vegetables from the grill and let cool. Cut the vegetables into ½-inch dice and set aside.
❋ In a large bowl, combine the tomatoes, cucumber, tomato juice, vinegar, garlic, the ⅓ cup olive oil, the 1 teaspoon salt and the ¼ teaspoon pepper. Season to taste with hot-pepper sauce; the mixture should be quite spicy. Stir in the grilled vegetables. Cover and refrigerate to chill thoroughly, at least 2 hours.
❋ To serve, ladle soup into bowls or mugs.
Serves 8

Tropical Fruit Salad
with Toasted-Coconut Crème Fraîche

1¼ cups packaged, grated coconut

4 cups diced pineapple

1 papaya, halved, seeded, peeled and diced

1 mango, halved, pitted, peeled and diced

1 banana, peeled and diced

3 tablespoons freshly squeezed lime juice

2 cups crème fraîche

Prepare this seasonal salad in your kitchen at home and transport in separate containers to serve on deck. You can make a topping similar to crème fraîche by stirring 4 teaspoons of sour cream into 2 cups of lightly whipped heavy cream.

☀ Preheat an oven to 250°F. Spread the coconut in a shallow pan and place in the oven. Bake, stirring occasionally, until lightly toasted, 12–15 minutes. Remove from the oven and let cool.
☀ In a large bowl, combine the pineapple, papaya, mango, banana and ½ cup of the toasted coconut. Add the lime juice and toss gently to coat evenly .
☀ In a small bowl, stir ½ cup of the remaining coconut into the crème fraîche.
☀ To serve, mound the fruit in a large serving bowl or in individual bowls. Top with a spoonful of the crème fraîche and sprinkle with the remaining ¼ cup coconut. Pass the remaining crème fraîche at the table.
Serves 6–8

Citron Pressé and Limonata

For Citron Pressé:

1 cup freshly squeezed lemon juice

8 cups tap water

granulated sugar

ice cubes

For Limonata:

1 cup granulated sugar

1 cup water

1 cup freshly squeezed lemon juice

8 cups club soda or carbonated mineral water

ice cubes

CITRON PRESSÉ:
☀ Pour an equal amount of the lemon juice in the bottom of tall glasses. Pour the water into a carafe and set out with bowls of the sugar and ice cubes. Invite guests to stir in water and then sugar to taste and then fill their glasses with ice.
Serves 8

LIMONATA:
☀ In a small saucepan over high heat, combine the sugar and water. Bring to a boil and stir just until the sugar dissolves and the liquid is clear. Remove from the heat and let cool completely. Divide the sugar syrup equally among tall glasses. Then add an equal amount of the lemon juice and club soda and stir to combine. Fill the glasses with ice and serve at once.
Serves 8

Tropical Fruit Salad, Citron Pressé and Limonata

Sunset Books gratefully acknowledges the assistance and support of many friends at Starbucks Coffee Company: Howard Schultz for his incredible vision; and Howard Behar, Dave Olsen and Harry Roberts for making this book possible. We would also like to thank Shirley Bartlett, Darlene Hartman, Karen Malody, Bill Moore, and all the Starbucks partners.

TEXT CREDITS

Recipes pages 40–43 by Sue White.

Minor text excerpts in this volume appear courtesy of the following publishers: Abelard Schuman, 11; The Tea & Coffee Trade Journal, 14; Vintage Books, 15; Penguin Books, 18 left; Random House, 18 right; Whereabouts Press, 22 left; Imprenta Lehmann & Cia, 22 right; Antigua Imprenta de Murguía, 26; University of Hawaii Press, 30 left.

ILLUSTRATION CREDITS

All illustrations by Martha Anne Booth except for the following: pages 8–31 borders by Diana Reiss-Koncar, maps by Kenn Backhaus. Additional thanks to Charles Mize.

PHOTOGRAPHY CREDITS

The publisher would like to thank the following photographers and organizations for permission to reproduce their photographs:
(Abbreviations: b=below, t=top)

Art Resource: 25
John Bull: 27
Comstock: Georg Gerster 10(b), Boyd Norton 17, 19
Courtesy of the San Francisco Library: 13
DDB Stock Photography: Suzanne L. Murphy 24
Robert Estall Photographs/Angela Fisher & Carol Beckwith: 9, 10(t)
Galería 1-2-3, El Salvador: 21
Collection of the Mexican Museum, San Francisco: 26(t), 26(b)
Nick Gunderson: 3, 31
Photo 20-20: Kimberly Parsons 23, Ann Cecil 30
Courtesy of the Kona Historical Society Archives: 28, 29
Scott Price: 5(b) & 8, 11
Philip Salaverry: 35, 36, 37(t), 37(b), 38
The Stock Market: Richard Steedman 12, Viviane Moos 14, Jose Fuste Raga 15, Luis Villota 16, 20

The photographer and stylist would like to thank the following (from San Francisco unless otherwise specified): Aude Bronson-Howard, NYC; Beaver Bros. Antiques; Cyclamen Studios Berkeley, Julie Sanders Designer; Crate and Barrel; Ward Finer; Judy and Bernie Carrasco; Bea and Marty Glenn; Rosie and Glenn-Finer; Merna Oeberst; Laura Newsom; Paul Bauer Inc.; Danial Schuster; Sue Fisher King; Virginia Breier Gallery; Beatrice Rosenberg; Spreck and Isabella Rosenkrans.